Title: Battle Plans

ISBN: 978-0615910185

DEDICATION

I dedicate this book to my Dad who was part of this nation's "Greatest Generation." Dad served our nation in WWII. He loved this country and the freedom it offers. To those who served in time of war, you know what it's like to put your life on the line for a cause greater than you. This is our life in Christ. We serve a cause greater than anything this world offers us. We serve a King, who was and is, and is to come.

In addition, I would like to thank the Reverend Bobby Dickey who showed me how to seek the Lord about my entangling sin. His insight helped me gain the freedom I longed for but could never attain. Once God set me free, He called me to help others find their freedom.

This study is the result of seeking God and learning how to teach others to free themselves from their entangling or addictive sins through Christ and the power of His Holy Spirit.

Just as our WWII vets fought for our freedom and settled for nothing less than victory, I found, if we are to experience the liberty we have in Christ, then we must have the same attitude toward an addiction.

Are you ready to fight for your freedom and win? I pray you are because when it comes to serving Christ, *Victory is the Only Option*.

TABLE OF CONTENTS

READINESS ALERT

Your mission is about to take place. As a Trusted Soldier, you will find yourself in a battle for your freedom. There is no going back, once you accept your challenge to enter this battle to win.

As always, victory is the only option, so you will need to have your mind, heart, and soul ready to engage the enemy. It won't be easy. The enemy is equipped for long-drawn out battles, so, you need to prepare for this battle through prayer and the mental preparedness it will take to win this war.

Before you begin this battle, you will need to create a mission statement. This statement will need to reflect your readiness and what you wish to attain once you have victory.

You are the Captain of your personal battle, so plan wisely and keep in touch with our Commander, the Lord, Jesus Christ.

God Speed on your adventure to take down Satan's hold on you. His stronghold is solidly entrenched in your territory, so you will have to be as wise as the old serpent to win this battle for your freedom.

Please make sure to pay close attention to your body armor and assets you have, while you learn how to identify the enemy's strengths and weaknesses and target his assets for destruction.

May God be with you in your endeavor.

THE PLEDGE

I chose the WWII solider to emulate because it was the last time America entered a war to win. When fighting an addiction, you must enter the battle to win. In addition, the Bible speaks of a *Good Soldier*, in 2 Timothy 3:5. The Good Soldier is one that endures difficulty and comes out a winner.

I created one other type of soldier; one that embodies the *Good Soldier's* characteristics and more. I call this solder, the *Trusted Soldier.* This soldier not only trusts God, but God can trust this soldier. It is a soldier who lives by faith in His Creator and will do all he can to win His internal battles, so he might become the man God created him to be.

When we're young, it seems like we will live forever. Then, life happens. And before we know it we're thirty, then forty. And then, we're sixty. Why waste this life with an addiction when Jesus wants to set you free through the power of the Holy Spirit?

In this *Battle Plans* study, you will learn who you are in Christ and the tactics it will take to win freedom's battle. Today, pledge to become a *Trusted Soldier* and enter the battle for your freedom to win. After all, the only option for the WWII soldier and the *Trusted Soldier* is victory.

God Bless! And may the victory God already provided for you, through Christ, become a reality in your life. *Because your freedom is the only option.*

THE PLEDGE

Today, I solemnly swear, as a Trusted Soldier of the kingdom God, to do all I can do to answer the call to fight for my liberty. I will follow the Battle Plan guide, and carry out my part to engage the enemy, in the power of the Lord. In the end, I want to experience the victory we already have in Him. Freedom is what I fight for and victory is the only option.

(Signature): _____   (Date): _____

KNOW YOUR MISSION

Providing an overview of your task is important. Begin by writing your mission statement defining the mission's goal in 30 words or less. While working through your battle plan, a quick review of your mission statement, before you begin each day, will help keep your focus centered on Christ and His mission for you.

Your mission statement may reflect God's call on your life and what He wants you to achieve through Him. It could also reflect what freedom means to you. A mission statement sets a goal or path for you to follow. Even God had a mission statement: "For God so loved the world, that he gave his only Son, that whoever believes in him should not perish but have eternal life" (John 3:16).

MISSISSION STATEMENT

Prayer: *Pray and seek God for your mission statement. Ask Him to make it clear and understandable to you. The Lord is your Commander. Therefore, call on Him to give you clarity regarding your life's journey.*

The End Game: *Your statement should point to your end-game. It should reflect who you are and what you want to become. The Lord says, "I am God, and there is none like me, declaring the end from the beginning and from ancient times things not yet done, saying, 'My counsel shall stand, and I will accomplish all my purpose...'" (Isaiah 46:9b-10).*

Sample Mission Statement I: from Pat Robertson: "I want to be part of God's plan of what He is doing on earth, and I want to bring Him glory."

Sample Mission Statement II: from Louise Morganti: "MY MISSION IN LIFE IS TO SERVE GOD BY BEING: A beacon of light, A bridge of understanding. A tower of integrity, and A castle of realized dreams.

Sample Mission Statement III: Our mission is to change hearts for the Lord.

Please write your sample mission statement. Some examples are on the previous page: Make sure it's what you wish to accomplish for the Lord or in life, after you experience your liberty through Christ. Try and keep it under 30 words.

_____

_____

_____

_____

_____

Signature: _____ Date:_____

DAY 2
KNOW YOUR WEAPONS

For the weapons of our warfare are not of the flesh but have divine power to destroy strongholds. 2 Corinthians 10:4

God doesn't expect us to fight our battles alone. Through Christ, we have many weapons at our disposal to take on Satan and his minions. What we need is a battle plan to freedom. To help you develop your plan, this study combines God's Word and military strategies from *The Art of War*, by Sun Tzu. Military experts consider it to be the most significant tactical handbook ever written. The tactics taught by Sun Tzu often reflect the teachings found in God's Word. I wrote this book because Satan uses military approaches to attack us. By studying military maneuvers and comparing them with scripture, you'll gain a better understanding about spiritual warfare where you can engage the enemy and put him on the run, so you may experience the victory you already have in Christ.

An addiction is difficult to overlook or dismiss. As the years roll by, these sins cause mental, physical, and spiritual suffering. What does Sun Tzu say about extended wars? He says, *"...men's weapons will grow dull and their ardor will be dampened."* In addition, a long, protracted war will sap the soldier's strength. (TAW) 2

When fighting Satan and his minions, a long, drawn-out clash with the demonic can blind you to the things of God. It can also quench God's Spirit where everything around you becomes dark. Long-term addictions will dull your sword (the Word of God) and undermine the spiritual armor you need to defend your mind and heart. Without a plan to defeat the enemy, you will remain vulnerable to Satan's temptations and accusations.

If you want to experience freedom, you must take time to study the truths found in God's Word and learn to use the tactics necessary to resist Satan. By standing on His

Word and walking in the power of the Holy Spirit, you will overcome the demonic influences in your life. As you read *Battle Plans*, know your freedom is worth the effort.

WEAPONS/ARMOR

Through Christ and the power of His Holy Spirit, you receive spiritual weapons and armor to stand against Satan and his dark forces. Read Ephesians 6:10-18.

BELT OF TRUTH

- From my perspective, the belt was the most important military piece the Romans had because their breastplate and how they maneuvered in battle relied on it. Roman soldiers used their belts to hold their breastplates tight. When they needed to maneuver in battle, they tucked their tunics in their belts. Likewise, the belt of truth is the most important weapon we have in our spiritual arsenal. Every armor piece we have relies on it.
- Learning truth is how we put our armor on. It also strengthens our helmet of salvation and our breastplate of righteousness.
- It sharpens and energizes our sword (the word), empowers our shield of faith, and causes our feet to stand firm as we travel throughout the world to share the Gospel, making disciples of all nations.
- Only the Truth (Jesus Christ), and His Word, will set us free. As we study and add more truth, truth enters our minds and hearts to protect us from our enemy's lies and temptations.
- As for the enemy, he knows how important truth is for a believer. His plan is to keep us enslaved to sin. He does this by trying to convince us there is no truth. Instead, Satan wants us to believe all truth is relative to a situation and not absolute. Thus, He cuts the belt of truth by claiming there is no truth. This tactic can leave us powerless to stand against him. To experience our freedom, we must know the truth because only the truth will set us free (John 8:32).

BREASTPLATE OF RIGHTEOUSNESS

- Ephesians 6:14 mentions the breastplate of righteousness. The breastplate of righteousness guards our heart to make sure it does not replace the truth with the world's lies. If a lie reaches our heart, it becomes us. Only Christ can destroy the lies embedded in our hearts and replace them with truth.
- As for the truth, it strengthens our breastplate and increases our faith.

SHOES FOR THE FEET

- God fits us with a readiness to share the Gospel of peace (Eph. 6:15).

- We are to share the Word in season and out of season. Studying the Word provides us a firm foundation to stand on and readies our feet to go and tell (2 Tim. 4:2).
- "But in your hearts revere Christ as Lord. Always be prepared to give an answer to everyone who asks you to give the reason for the hope that you have. But do this with gentleness and respect..." 1 Peter 3:15
- "For I am not ashamed of the gospel, for it is the power of God for salvation to everyone who believes..." (Romans 1:16).
- We are not ashamed of our Lord or the Gospel. Just as a soldier has confidence in his battle plan, we have the same confidence in God's plan; for the Good News is "the power of God for salvation to everyone who believes." Thus, our shoes symbolize our readiness to share the Gospel of Jesus Christ with the lost in this world.

HELMET OF SALVATION

- Our helmet protects our heads and minds from the devil's temptations, accusations, and lies (Eph. 6:17).
- The more truth we have, the stronger the helmet's protection.
- Truth renews our minds on Christ. It also allows us to stand against Satan's attacks on our thought-life.

SWORD OF THE SPIRIT

- The sword of the Spirit represents God's Word. When we know God's Word, we can use it to stand against Satan's accusations and temptations. The sword's strength comes from the truths found in God's Word (Eph. 6:17).
- "For the Word of God is living and active, sharper than any two-edged sword, piercing to the division of soul and of spirit, of joints and of marrow, and discerning the thoughts and intentions of the heart." Hebrews 4:12

THE SHIELD OF FAITH

- Faith separates the mature in the faith from young believers and the saved from the unsaved. Without it, we cannot please God, nor can we experience salvation. Faith, our shield mentioned in Ephesians 6:16, allows us to fend off doubts and fears. It gives us the courage we need to survive life's unexpected trials. Even when we fail to see ourselves as free by faith, we must want to be free and trust God to do the rest.
- "Now faith is the assurance of things hoped for, the conviction of things not seen." Hebrews 11:1
- "That is why it depends on faith, in order that the promise may rest on grace and be guaranteed to all his offspring—not only to the adherent of the law but also to the one who shares the faith of Abraham, who is the father of us all..." Romans 4:16

- Not that we lord it over your faith, but we work with you for your joy, for you stand firm in your faith." 2 Corinthians 1:24
- "...and everything that does not come from faith is sin." Romans 14:23
- "...if we are faithless, he remains faithful—for he cannot deny himself." Even when we have moments of doubt or we come to believe God doesn't love us anymore, He remains faithful toward us, even when we are faithless. (2 Tim. 2:13)

PRAYING IN THE SPIRIT

- What does it mean to pray in the Spirit? My brother used to describe it as praying through to God's throne.
- The way to communicate with God is through the spirit. When we pray in the spirit, the Holy Spirit enables us to understand the Word and hear the Lord. This way, we can pray about what God places on our hearts (1 Cor. 2:13-14).
- What if we cannot hear God or find the words to pray? Romans 8:26 says, "Likewise the Spirit helps us in our weakness. For we do not know what to pray for as we ought, but the Spirit himself intercedes for us with groaning's too deep for words."

LOVE

- "It (love) always protects, always trusts, always hopes, always perseveres." 1 Corinthians 13:7
- "But I say to you, love your enemies and pray for those who persecute you..." Doing these can help you win over your enemies with love (Matt. 5:44).
- "The love of Christ compels us to change our lives, where we want to do right." 2 Corinthians 5:14
- "The aim of our charge is love that issues from a pure heart and a good conscience and a sincere faith." 1 Timothy 1:5
- "Above all, love one another earnestly, since love covers a multitude of sins." 1 Peter 4:8

GOD, OUR SHIELD AND FORTRESS

The Word says, "...he is my steadfast love and my fortress, my stronghold and my deliverer, my shield and he in whom I take refuge, who subdues peoples under me." Psalm 144:2

TAKING INVENTORY OF YOUR ARMOR/WEAPONS

Soldiers fight their enemies using the weapons they have at their disposal. When fighting Satan's temptations and overcoming sin, knowing what strengthens our weapons and how we use them in battle are necessary if we want to remain free in Christ. On the next page, please list and give a short description of the armor you would like to have God strengthen, so you can use your armor effectively.

TAKING INVENTORY

> *The Words "be strong," describes the act of strengthening or to strengthen. As we mature in Christ, we grow stronger in faith and greater in courage. We accomplish these by dying to ourselves and coming closer to Jesus. In dying to ourselves, we let the Lord know we cannot quit on our own. Because of our many failures, we recognize Jesus is the only answer to our freedom.*

God gives us a measure of faith (Rom. 12:3), and He emboldens us through His Holy Spirit, so we might experience victory over our sins. Therefore, as we become weaker, He becomes stronger. His might and power, found in the Holy Spirit, will give us the victory.

KNOW YOURSELF

OUR TRANSFORMATION IN CHRIST

Soldiers enter basic training as individuals and leave as members of a team committed to defending their homeland. No longer able to do their own will, they answer to their superiors and carry out their will.

After basic training, soldiers receive special training to help their military branch carry out its mission. Wherever their country needs them to serve, they will heed the call to protect the homeland by following orders and carrying out their assigned mission.

GOD'S PLANS FOR HIS PEOPLE

"For those whom he foreknew he also predestined to be conformed to the image of his Son, in order that he might be the firstborn among many brothers" (Rom. 8:29). Just as the military trains individuals to become part of a professional fighting team, God does the same for us. He saves us and plants us into the functioning body of Christ to carry out His will and pleasure to expand His kingdom. Serving Christ, we no longer do our will but His (Gal. 2:20).

CHANGES THAT TAKE PLACE THROUGH SALVATION:

- Cleansed mind, heart of flesh, new Spirit (Ezek. 36:25-26).
- Crucified the old man; freed from the power of sin and death, justified (Rom. 6:6-7).
- Dead to the law. It no longer has the authority to condemn us. (Rom. 7:1-6).
- Under grace. Grace reigns in our lives (Rom. 5:20-21).
- New creation in Christ (2 Cor. 5:17).
- Offers forgiveness for our sins. Because Christ paid the penalty, we have forgiveness for all our sins, past, present and future. (1 Jn. 2:12, Rom. 4:7).
- Justified by of our faith in Christ; God declares us righteous in His eyes (Rom. 5:1, Acts 13:39).

- The Holy Spirit allows us to understand the things of God (1 Cor. 2:10-15).
- God adopts us as His children by faith in Christ (Rom. 8:15).
- Redeemed or purchased by the blood of Christ (Eph. 1:7, Col. 1:14, 1 Cor. 7:23, 1 Cor. 6:20).
- No longer slaves to sin (Rom. 6:20).
- We place ourselves under His authority and walk in His righteousness (Rom.6:22).
- Christ defeated death. Because of this, we no longer live under a death sentence (Rom. 6:23, Gal. 3:13).
- Because of Christ, we become spiritual descendants of Abraham (Rom. 9:7-8).
- Inheritors of eternal life (John 3:16-17).

The above changes occur through salvation. We are no longer who we were before Christ. We are new creations. Old things have passed away and everything becomes new (2 Cor. 5:17). What does this mean to you? The demonic wants you to think nothing has changed. Although, the addiction you had before you came to Christ may remain, you now have the power to destroy it.

> The Word says, "For we know that our old self was crucified with him so that the body ruled by sin might be done away with, that we should no longer be slaves to sin— because anyone who has died has been set free from sin" (Rom. 6:6-7).

Christ put your old nature to death by crucifying it. Your new nature is righteousness. Having a new nature, you no longer need to continue in sin. Letting this idea sink in allows you to stand against your sin from a strong, spiritual position as opposed to using your *will* as your only defense. Understanding you no longer need to continue to sin is an important first step in defeating your addiction.

A transformation happened when we came to Christ. In fact, we are to profess this change by faith. Romans 6:11 says, "In the same way, count yourselves dead to sin but alive to God in Christ Jesus." To experience this transformation, a mind-set change must take place within. Realizing what happened through Christ, we go from believing we are a helpless sinner to knowing the cross crucified the old man and set us free from the power of sin (the law). Because of this, we tell ourselves, "We don't have to commit this sin anymore." Declaring your independence from your sin acknowledges the mind-set change. It will propel you to experience a life of freedom in Christ, for Christ defeated both the power of sin [the law] and the sting of sin [death] (1 Cor. 15:56).

PLEASE ANSWER THE FOLLOWING:

Explain what being a new creation means to you:

_____

_____

_____

Learning what takes place within you, how can these changes help you in your struggles with sin? Please explain.

_____

_____

_____

Based on Romans 6:6-7 and 6:11, describe the mind-set change that took place in you. Let this mindset become you. Knowing this puts you on your path to freedom. So, take time to declare your independence below.

_____

_____

_____

_____

_____

YOUR CHARACTERISTICS

YOUR CHARACTERISTICS CHART

CHARACTERISTIC	YES	NO
God's love expressed through you to others:		
Forgive others easily:		
Hold a grudge:		
Use foul language:		
Yes means "Yes":		
No means "No":		
Humble:		
Prideful:		
Jealous:		
Difficulty telling the truth:		
Blame others for your mistakes:		
Take responsibility for your actions:		
Lie to yourself or to protect yourself:		
Difficulty keeping Promises:		

Feel trapped by your sin:		
Anger Issues:		
Pray occasionally:		
Pray daily – a prayer warrior:		
Study God's Word regularly:		
Witness to others:		
Gossip:		
Teach others:		
Use your will to overcome sin:		
Seek God when making major decisions:		
Regularly thank God:		
Regularly praise God outside the church:		
Believe your addiction is just part of who you are:		
Goal setter:		
Know God's will for your life:		
Have assurance of your salvation:		
Believe you can lose your salvation:		
Feel forgiven:		
People can trust you to keep a secret.		
Experience answered prayer:		
God can trust you with the little things:		
Easily ensnared or enslaved by sin:		
Lead a Bible study:		
Want to be free to serve Christ:		
Guided by the Spirit:		
Want to know His will:		
Seek wealth, fame power:		

After examining your weaknesses and strengths, please take time to write, on a separate piece of paper, where you need to improve. Think about how these improvements may help you in your walk with God, and your interaction with other believers.

KNOW YOUR SPIRITUAL GIFT

God gives us spiritual gifts to serve His kingdom. Know your spiritual gift by visiting the following link and taking the Spiritual Gift Inventory for yourself: http://www.churchgrowth.org/cgi-cg/gifts.cgi?intro=1 .

Note: While this test may not be perfect and solely relies on your answers, it is accurate if you are honest with yourself when answering these questions.

According to the test what is your strongest gift? _____

What is your secondary gift? _____

What is your weakest gift? _____

How can knowing your gifts help you better serve the Lord Jesus?

_____

_____

_____

DAY 5
KNOW YOUR ENEMIES

THE WORLD

God created the world for us to enjoy. As God's ambassadors to this world, we are not to adopt the world's ways. Jesus said His kingdom is not of this world and neither is ours (John 18:36). He explained how anyone who loves their life will lose it, and anyone who hates their life will live in eternity with Christ. This does not mean we hate living. It means we do not place our hope in this life. And if called on, we will lay down our lives for the cause of Christ (John 12:25).

Trusted soldiers never entangle themselves with this world. This means they do not buy into the world's systems, nor do they participate in the sinful deeds the world calls normal behavior. Instead, they remain guided by a higher law in service of the Lord, Jesus Christ.

When we fail to obey the Lord or His Word, we fall under our Father's discipline (Heb.12:5-13). For true believers, thinking what happens if we fail to carry out God's will because we allowed an addiction to sidetrack or disqualify us is too frightening to consider. Paul writes, "So I do not run aimlessly; I do not box as one beating the air. But I discipline my body and keep it under control, lest after preaching to others I myself should be disqualified (1 Cor. 9:26-27).

The lost do not know Christ nor do they understand God (John 14:17). These people love the things of this world and accept the ungodly desires the world has to offer. Because they do not have the Spirit, they cannot understand the spiritual. For their human spirit, void of the Holy Spirit, can only understand the things of the flesh. Because of this, the things from the Spirit of God sound foolish to them (1 Cor. 2:10-16). Jesus said, "If you were of the world, it would love you as its own. As it is, you are not of the world, but I have chosen you out of the world. That is why the world hates you" (John 15:19 NIV). He also said, "And this is the judgment: the light has come into the world, and people loved the darkness rather than the light because their works were evil" (John 3:19).

THE FUTILITY IN TRYING TO GAIN THE ENTIRE WORLD

While the worldly try to succeed by grabbing power, seeking fame, or heaping riches on themselves, Jesus reminds us how unprofitable it is for us to gain the world and lose our souls (Matt. 16:26). People who seek these cannot see how addictive their pursuit of these can become. If they are not careful, the things of this world become their sole purpose in life. And when they die, what do they have left? Nothing. As Paul writes, "We brought nothing into this world, and we can take nothing with us" (1Tim. 6:7).

WISDOM OF THIS WORLD

First Corinthians 3:19 tells us the wisdom of this world is foolishness compared to the wisdom we have in Christ. The world sees us as peculiar people (1 Pe. 2:9) They may even see us as a threat to their way of life; referring to us as hypocrites, haters, and intolerant people.

They hate us because we stand against the sinful pleasures of this world by submitting ourselves to a higher authority along with the truths found in God's Word. These people do not believe in absolutes such as God's Word or Jesus Christ who is the living Truth. Instead, they believe the individual establishes their own truths and every truth is relative to a situation.

SATAN BLINDS THE WORLD

The god of this world blinds unbelievers. He tries to make it impossible for them to see the light. Yet, the Spirit of God is greater than the powers of darkness. The Holy Spirit breaks through the spiritual darkness unbeliever's face and enables them to see the light of Christ in us (2 Cor. 4:4).

RENOUNCING UNGODLINESS

As Trusted Soldiers, we are to renounce ungodliness, along with our worldly passions, so we might become faithful believers God can trust to carry out His kingdom plans on earth. For willful sin is blasphemy in God's eyes (Num. 15:30). In addition, we are to remain self-controlled and upright by living our lives to reflect our Commander, Jesus Christ (Titus 2:12). James said those who buy into the world's system and seek its evil pleasures are God's enemies (Jas. 4:4). Peter said, "For if, after they have escaped the defilements of the world through the knowledge of our Lord and Savior Jesus Christ, they are again entangled in them and overcome, the last state has become worse for them than the first" (2 Pe. 2:20).

John writes, "For all that is in the world—the desires of the flesh and the desires of the eyes and pride of life—is not from the Father but is from the world" (1 Jn. 2:16). He warns us about loving the world. If a person loves it, "the love of the Father is not in him" (1 Jn. 2:15).

We know Jesus will return to this world one day. When Christ returns, will you feel joy or shame? It's not something most of us think about but we should because the rewards we receive or lose in heaven depend on the work we do on earth.

Please list the factors or things you believe keep you from submitting yourself to Christ.

_____

_____

_____

_____

THE FLESH

We are flesh, soul, and spirit. Our flesh is our outer covering. The Spirit lives in our human spirit and enables us to hear God (1 Cor. 2:10-15). We also have a soul. It contains our mind and heart. The soul makes it possible for us to think and feel. It also defines us.

When the Word speaks of the flesh, in terms of sin, it's not talking about our outer covering. No, it's talking about the "flesh principle." We find this principle, called the law of sin, in Romans 7:25. The Word says, "...but I see in my members another law waging war against the law of my mind and making me captive to the law of sin that dwells in my members" (Rom. 7:23). While we remain in our bodies, this law exists. We should never allow the law of sin to enslave us. Instead, the Bible commands us to flee from sin, put it to death, or cut it off.

We can run from some sins because we know better and have the power within us to resist them (1 Cor. 6:18, 10:14, 1 Tim. 6:11, 2 Tim. 2:2). Then, there are those sins and activities we cut-off voluntarily because they may influence others to do the same (Matt. 5:29-30). For instance, I gave up drinking to honor God and my children. I found it easy to do because I was not addicted to alcohol. As for our addictive or entangling sins, we must seek the Lord to have the Holy Spirit put these desires to death. If we don't, these sins will enslave our hearts and minds (Col. 3:5, Rom. 8:13).

We mentioned how the Word divides sin into three categories: The pride of life, the lust of the flesh, and the lust of the eyes (1 Jn. 2:16). These sins will take us down and hinder our walk with God. Therefore, walk with the wisdom of God. If you battle with pride, you must be careful because pride can lead you to fall sooner than later. If you suffer the lust of the eyes, then ask God to give you eyes for your spouse only, just as Job did (Job 31:1). Another is the lust of the flesh. This sin derails many Christians. We address how to overcome this throughout the workbook.

THE DESTRUCTIVENESS OF AN ENSLAVING, ADDICTIVE SIN

I remember reading about a counselor who refuse to gamble with his friends. One day, his friends convinced him gambling was nothing more than entertainment, so he headed to the casinos with them. At first, he set limits on what he allowed himself to lose. Over time, those limits faded away. Without the limits, he lost his savings, his retirement, and his home.

This man had the desire to gamble and waited for the right excuse to join his friends. Being an addiction counselor, he thought he could beat the odds and not become addicted. What he thought he could control, controlled him. And what he toyed with, in his mind, became a reality; and it cost him everything he had (Jas. 1:13-15).

Below, list the sins you struggle with.

_____

_____

_____

_____

THE DARK FORCES

I won't spend a great deal of time on Satan because we take an extensive look at him in the next section. But, there are a few characteristics I'd like to point out: First, Satan is real. Next, Satan is a powerful being. Third, he tempts us and makes accusations toward us. Fourth, Satan is a liar. Fifth, he wants to steal our joy in the Lord, kill our witness, and destroy our life (1 Pe. 5:8). Finally, he blinds the world to the Gospel, making it impossible for them to understand it (2 Cor 4:4).

God allows Satan to roam the earth and accuse believers before His throne. He also lets Satan tempt us. Satan performs these deceitful and treacherous acts with great skill and forethought, then accuses us when we bite. (Zech. 3:1-3, Rev.12:10). Without Christ, we would have no chance to defeat him. But with Christ, we can stop the temptations and accusations through the power of the Holy Spirit working in us to free us from our sinful desires.

BINDING AND LOOSING

I tell you the truth, whatever you bind on earth will be bound in heaven, and whatever you loose on earth will be loosed in heaven (Matthew 18:18).

Many believers think Matthew 18:18 gives us the authority to bind Satan on earth. If we could bind Satan, we would never have to worry about him again. Imagine over 2 billion believers using their authority, in Christ, to constrain Satan. He would spend his entire time trying to free himself from all the non-stop, binding aimed at him. Looking at this from a logical perspective, you can see why God never gave us the right to constrain him. It's true, God will bind him one day but for now, God uses Satan to perform those things He will never because of His holiness. For example, God uses temptations to test our hearts. God cannot tempt us, so he allows Satan to do it (Jas. 1:10-15). Even with all his power and treacherous behavior, our Heavenly Father limits the damage Satan can inflict upon us (Job 1).

If you read Matt.18:18 in context, God gives the early church leadership authority to deal with sin and interpret God's Word where clarity is needed. Remember, the early church did not have a New Testament to guide them. God granted authority for the Apostles to come up with some answers. Whatever they concluded on earth, God bound or accepted in heaven.

Some examples where the church needed clarification:

- Salvation by Faith alone.
- The edict against Gentile Circumcision
- Gentiles should not eat meat from sacrificed or strangled animals.
- They should not take part in sexual immorality.

Below, list some works you have either done for the Lord or would like to do because God placed these desires on your heart.

_____

_____

_____

_____

SATAN'S CHARACTERISTICS

SATAN'S STRENGTHS

We need to define our enemies if we are to put Satan and his demons on the run. To defeat them, we should learn their tactics, understand their strengths, and know their weaknesses and limitations.

> *The Word defines our enemies. It says, "For our struggle is not against flesh and blood, but against the rulers, against the authorities, against the powers of this dark world and against the spiritual forces of evil in the heavenly realms" (Eph. 6:12).*

A LIST OF OUR ENEMIES

- Are not flesh and blood. They are spiritual beings.
- Rulers, authorities, and powers of this dark world.
- Spiritual forces of evil residing in the heavenly realms.

OUR ENEMY OPERATES IN THE FOLLOWING WAYS

On the next page, read the list of strengths Satan possess and check "Yes" if Satan or his demons have used one or more against you or "No" if they haven't. As you read these, you will see how the enemy affects the way you think and act. Satan is cunning in all his ways. If you want to experience victory over the demonic, you must know your enemy's tactics and what he can and cannot do.

SATAN'S STRENGTHS[3]	YES	NO
He is like a roaring lion – prowling around, looking for someone to devour (1 Pe. 5:8).		
Satan will disguise himself as an angel of light (2 Cor. 11:14).		
Satan, full of pride, wants to be like God (Ezek. 28:1-2).		
Satan is the father of lies—it's his character (John 8:44).		
Satan is a murderer (John 8:44).		
Satan is the deceiver (Gen. 3:1-5, Rev. 12:9).		
Satan is the accuser of those who believe in Christ. (Rev. 12:10).		
He hinders our prayers (Dan. 10:12-13).		
He hinders God's servants and the work they do (1Thes. 2:18).		
He afflicts God's people (Job 2:7).		
Satan blinds the minds of unbelievers. (2 Cor. 4:4).		
He interferes with the sanctity of the home (adultery, addiction, lies).		
Satan afflicts people in general (Job 2:7, Luke, 13:16, Acts 10:38).		
He causes us to feel discouragement (1 Sam. 30:6).		
Satan causes us to feel despair (2 Cor. 4:8).		
Satan causes us to become bewitched (Gen. 3:1).		
He causes us to feel distracted (Matt. 14:30).		
He leads us to become double-minded in all our ways (Matt. 6:24).		

It's important to know how Satan uses his strengths against you. By understanding how Satan attacks, you can engage him with the weapons God gave you to defeat him.

EVALUATION

Please review *Satan's Strengths*. Did you know the thoughts you have are often from Satan? Did you think they were your own thoughts? Take the time to review the list. Then pray over them. Ask God to remove Satan's influence over your life. When you pray, try including these words, "Father, lead me not into temptation, but deliver me from Satan's attacks on my life by killing the desire for my sin, so I might walk in liberty and become the person you created me to be. Amen!"

SATAN'S LIMITATIONS [4]

If we want to defeat Satan or one of his minions, we should learn their limitations and weaknesses. Many people engage Satan and his demons without understanding them. When engaging an enemy, we should avoid their strengths, exploit their limitations, and attack their weak spots. If we want to win this war, we should use this knowledge to our advantage.

> *"Hence, a skillful fighter puts himself into a position which makes defeat possible, and does not miss the moment for defeating the enemy."* [(TAW) 5] *Sun Tzu*

- Satan is not omnipresent. He cannot be everywhere. Satan travels back and forth, throughout the world, to see whom he can devour (Read Job 1).
- Satan is not omniscient. He does not know everything, nor does he have infinite knowledge about our thoughts, feelings, character, our lives, life in general, or the universe. Nor does he have infinite knowledge and wisdom about all God's plans. For instance, Satan thought he defeated Jesus until Sunday came.
- Satan is not omnipotent. He is not all-powerful. His strength is useless against our Lord (John 12:31, 16:11).
- Sin corrupted Satan's wisdom. He thought he could be equal with God (Ezek.28:17, Isa. 14:12-14).
- God is Sovereign, not Satan. God limits Satan in his ability to attack the saints and the severity of the attacks against God's people (Job 1:1-8).

SATAN'S WEAKNESSES [6]

- When tempting us, God will never allow Satan to go beyond what we can handle in Christ (1 Cor. 10:13).
- Satan's lies cannot stand against God's Word (Luke 4:1-13).
- Demons tremble at the name of Jesus (Jas. 2:19).
- Satan is a defeated foe; the prince of this world already stands legally judged (John 16:11).
- He cannot resist a believer who humbles himself and stands against him (Jas. 4:7).
- Satan cannot withstand Christ's blood or a saint's testimony (Rev. 12:11).
- He cannot continue to accuse us once the Lord frees us from our entangling sins (Zech. 3:1).

VICTORIOUS IN BATTLE

> *Thus, to be successful in battle, "The consummate leader cultivates the moral law and strictly adheres to the method of discipline."* (TAW) 7 *Sun Tzu*

Paul reminds us how important our moral standing is to our walk with God. He writes, "But I discipline my body and keep it under control, lest after preaching to others I myself should be disqualified" (1 Cor. 9:27).

> *"Making no mistakes is what establishes the certainty of victory, for it means conquering an enemy that is already defeated."* (TAW) 8 *Sun Tzu*

Remember, Satan is a defeated foe (John 12:31, 16:11). Jesus already did the work. We need to remind the devil of this when standing against him and his demonic forces in the name of Christ.

> *"If you know your enemy and you know yourself you need not fear the result of a hundred battles. If you know yourself and not the enemy, for every victory you gained, you will also suffer defeat. If you know neither the enemy nor yourself, you will succumb in every battle."* (TAW) 9 *Sun Tzu*

John 8:44 says, "You are of your father the devil, and your will is to do your father's desires. He was a murderer from the beginning, and has nothing to do with the truth, because there is no truth in him. When he lies, he speaks out of his own character, for he is a liar and the father of lies."

Paul says, "...so that we would not be outwitted by Satan; for we are not ignorant of his designs" (2 Cor. 2:11).

First Peter 5:8 tells us to remain vigilant and clear-minded when dealing with Satan or one of his demons. Peter issues the following warning. He says, "be sober-minded; be watchful. Your adversary the devil prowls around like a roaring lion, seeking someone to devour" (1 Pe. 5:8).

LIMITING YOUR EXPOSURE TO HIS DEVICES

How can it help you know Satan's strengths, limitations, and weaknesses?

_____

_____

_____

_____

_____

DAY 7

KNOW THE BATTLEFIELD

God told Solomon he could ask for anything from God, and He would give it to him. What did the king ask God to give him? He said, "Give your servant therefore an understanding mind to govern your people, that I may discern between good and evil, for who is able to govern this, your great people?" (1Kings 3:9). God honored Solomon with great wisdom. In fact, no one, other than our Lord, has had the wisdom to match Solomon's wisdom.

So, where do our battles take place? They take place in our mind; "For the desires of the flesh are against the Spirit, and the desires of the Spirit are against the flesh, for these are opposed to each other…" (Gal. 5:17).

During WWII, commanders did their best to know what they were about to face on the battlefield and accounted for this ahead of time. Our military leaders did their best to leave nothing to chance. While they couldn't prevent every attack or loss of life, soldiers used their intuition and training to adapt to any surprises and mistakes they had to deal with in battle. No battle or war plan was perfect but knowing the terrain, the enemy, and using a soldier's ability to adapt to unexpected circumstances made the difference between winning and losing.

Satan, and his dark forces want to keep our minds under attack to prevent us from thinking good thoughts or giving praises to our Lord. So, it's up to us to remain focused on Christ and make sure Satan and his demons fail.

CALLED TO BE FREE

The Word says, "we all once lived in the passions of our flesh, carrying out the desires of the body and the mind, and were by nature children of wrath, like the rest of mankind" (Eph. 2:3). When we do not understand what freedom is like, we remain vulnerable to Satan's devices.

Years ago, the enemy tried to destroy me. Before the Lord set me free from my evil desires, I remember thinking, "God you need to accept me this way. I cannot change. I hate what I have become. I want to change, but nothing works. Since you won't let me experience freedom from my sin, then you will have to forgive me for being this way." And while these were not my exact words, they reflect my thought process. I didn't understand what freedom felt like. I read about it, but I never experienced it as a Christian. Evil thoughts held my mind captive for years. Rushing through my mind, with a hurricane-like force, these thoughts tore up every good thought, praise, or prayer I tried to offer to God.

Satan knows if we ever experience freedom, we will know the difference, and we will never want to return to our old ways. For this reason, the devil works overtime to keep us pinned down, so we remain enslaved to our addiction.

FREEDOM IS WORTH FIGHTING FOR

The battles fought in WWII were about preserving freedom. Our parents and grandparents loved freedom. Their generation never suffered a divided nation as we do today. They defended this land and died for the freedoms they enjoyed. For they would have never thought about selling out their freedom for security. It was freedom or nothing; no compromise or Plan B was acceptable. At the end of World War II, our dead and wounded totaled over 300,000. The only other war where we suffered more American casualties was the Civil War because Americans fought Americans.

Those brave soldiers went to war to protect our nation's freedoms. They loved their freedom and would not have allowed a nation to enslave us or our allies. When battling an addiction, we need to have the same attitude toward our personal freedom. Once the Holy Spirit puts our desire for sin to death, we will experience freedom. When we do, we need to defend it against Satan's attacks and never let it go.

In Second Corinthians 11:13 we read, "But I am afraid that as the serpent deceived Eve by his cunning, your thoughts will be led astray from a sincere and pure devotion to Christ." Satan entices us to justify our behavior. He plays on our emotions and lusts. He wants us to believe nothing changed after we received Christ. But, we know better. We no longer have a desire to sin. Instead, we want to experience our freedom in Christ, but we have no idea how to with this battle for our minds and hearts.

JUSTIFYING OUR SINS BEFORE A HOLY GOD

Some believers think grace allows them to sin without consequences. They believe God will forgive them because they have grace. Yes, God will forgive them, but the consequences for their sinful actions will cause them to reap the devastation sin brings upon them. Instead of accepting their fate and living with their guilt and shame, they must enter the battle, because freedom is worth the fight. It allows us to live with a clear conscience and follow Christ with joy and gladness.

While you struggle to taste freedom, remember what Job said, "For he will complete what he appoints for me, and many such things are in his mind" (Job 23:14). God will complete His work in you. He gives us this promise. The Lord will not allow those wicked thoughts to remain. Because you are His, the Lord, through the power of His Spirit working in you, can set you free. As you learn how, it's up to you to seek your freedom and allow God to do His work in you. You can no longer claim ignorance. You must choose to enter this battle and fight to overcome your enslaving sin.

FREEDOM IS THE ONLY OPTION

Attaining freedom, through victory, is our only option. We must free our minds from those wicked thoughts the demonic uses against us. We cannot win this battle in our own strength. The victory is the Lords. By trusting in your own efforts and your own reasoning, you will fail. Solomon writes, "Whoever trusts in his own mind is a fool, he who walks in wisdom will be delivered" (Prov. 28:26).

FIGHTING ON DESPERATE GROUND

Our mind and the heart play an important part in our victory. We must guard our minds by not allowing our evil thoughts to move from our mind to our heart. Once these thoughts reach our hearts, they become us. And while the battle rages in our mind, remember, Satan cannot have our soul (mind and heart), but He can influence it.

As Christians, we should not allow ourselves to remain double-minded. We are to love the Lord and have the mind of Christ, so we may experience Him in Spirit and truth. If not, we will remain double-minded, hoping to find something we already have (victory), but cannot attain.

> *Sun Tzu says, "Ground on which we can only be saved from destruction by fighting without delay is desperate ground."* (TAW) 10

The Word says, "We destroy arguments and every lofty opinion raised against the knowledge of God, and take every thought captive to obey Christ..." (2 Cor. 10:5). Our mind is the battlefield. It is desperate ground. So, we must prepare to engage the enemy and win the battle by capturing every evil thought attacking our minds. We should not let our minds receive those thoughts. Instead, we capture every evil thought and destroy them by casting them out or rebuking them with the Word of God and the name of Jesus. Because of the large number of attacks, you face, destroying these won't be easy. But you can do it. Over time, the attacks will end. Is this strategy worth it? Paul, Sun Tzu, and I say it is.

DAY 8

PLEASE THE COMMANDER

According to Second Timothy 2:4, we are to please our commanding officer. How do we please our Commander? We delight the Lord when we obey Him, trust Him, and have faith in Him. It must thrill the Lord when we finally give up who we are and follow His will for our lives.

Good soldiers never become entangled with the world. Instead, they serve their country and please their commander by following orders. When we remain entangled, we are not living to please the Lord. Of course, He loves us. His love is conditional based on our goodness. If you think about it, the Word says we have nothing to offer God in the flesh and so we fall short of His glory (Rom. 3:23). While our sins never affect our position, they can affect the relationship we have with Him.

A child can tell his parents he loves them with his lips, but his obedience or lack of it proves how much or how little he loves and respects them. God is no different. The Word says, "This people honors me with their lips, but their heart is far from me" (Matt. 15:8).

Jesus said, "You are my friends if you do what I command you" (John 15:14). Do you see how important our obedience is to our relationship with Christ? While He expects obedience from His soldiers, we often fall short. For this reason, we need grace. Jesus wants us to trust Him, walk in faith, and believe He can do what He promises us.

We can say Jesus is our friend, but it means nothing until He calls us friend. How do we know when Jesus calls us friend? Jesus says, "No longer do I call you servants, for the servant does not know what his master is doing; but I have called you friends, for all that I have heard from my Father I have made known to you" (John 15:15). Jesus entrusts His friends with the deeper truths from the Father, found in His Word.

THE WORD IS OUR MILITARY MANUAL

Every soldier receives a military manual. This manual teaches them the military codes of conduct. We also have a manual to follow. We call it the Bible. It tells us what God loves and hates. The Word gives us rules to live by and spiritual truths to walk in as we learn to grow in faith. Our Bibles tells us how to engage the enemy, so we might be victorious and experience our peace, joy, and freedom in Christ.

In Hebrews 11, we read about the men and women God honored. He honored them because of their faithfulness and their willingness to obey and trust Him. These are God's Medal of Honor winners; godly examples of how we are to live our lives. To be a faithful and trusted soldier, we must not remain entangled. We are to separate ourselves from unclean things in our lives by honoring Him with our lips and our hearts. When we obey the Lord, it pleases Him.

The Psalmist writes, "Praise the Lord! Praise God in his sanctuary; praise him in his mighty heavens! Praise him for his mighty deeds; praise him according to his excellent greatness!" (Psa. 150:1-2). In Ps.134:2 we read, "Lift up your hands to the holy place and bless the LORD!" We are to lift holy hands to the Lord. Are you lifting holy hands to Him? Yes, His holiness is in you. Because His blood covers you, you have the forgiveness of sin; but are you lifting holy hands to praise Him, or are you lifting the hands you use in darkness to carry out your entangling sin?

THE CONSEQUENCES OF OUR DISOBEDIENCE

In 1 Samuel 15, Saul became anxious waiting for the Prophet Samuel to offer a sacrifice to God before Saul and his soldiers could engage in battle. His soldiers had become fearful of the enemy, and many had already deserted him. Thinking Samuel was running late, Saul convinced himself he couldn't wait any longer. And so, he performed the sacrifice instead of Samuel. After Samuel arrived, he heard what Saul did and questioned the king's loyalty and obedience to God. He told Samuel, "Behold, to obey is better than sacrifice, and to listen than the fat of rams" (1 Sam. 15:22).

Saul thought his sacrifice would please God, but it didn't. Because he disobeyed God, Saul would lose his right to the throne. Rather than listen to Samuel, Saul panicked and caved to his own desires. In the same manner, we miss God's best for our life when we ignore Him and do what pleases us.

TRUST, OBEDIENCE, AND FAITH PLEASES OUR COMMANDER

We must have faith in the Lord's promises and trust He will bring about His plan and purpose for our lives. In Psalm 18:30 we read, "This God—his way is perfect; the word of the LORD (His promises) proves true…" Thus, if the Lord gives you a promise, through His Word or His still, small voice, you can trust it. For the Lord cannot lie.

> "The Moral Law causes the people to be in complete accord with their ruler, so they will follow him regardless of their lives, undismayed by danger." *(TAW 11)*

Our Lord says, "If anyone would come after me, let him deny himself and take up his cross and follow me. For whoever would save his life will lose it, but whoever loses his life for my sake and the gospel's will save it" (Mark 8:34-35).

Remember, our faith pleases God. Even when our faith fails, He remains faithful (2 Tim. 2:13). So, trust in the Lord, walk in faith, obey Him, and become the person God called you to be in this world. Your goal is to please your Commander. Is your walk pleasing to Him?

Write the three most important changes you need to make to please the Lord and become a living sacrifice to Him.

_____

_____

_____

Now is the time to praise the Lord and thank Him in advance for the victory you are about to see expressed in your life. Ask Him to give you the faith to believe in His promises, so you might experience the peace, joy, and freedom God has for you in Christ.

DAY 9

LINE OF COMMUNICATION

A soldier's line of communication is important to his success. If a mission is to succeed, good communications between the front line and support is necessary to gain victory. As Christians, our success depends on having a line of communication between headquarters or heaven and us. Prayer is how we connect with God. Because God sees everything, it's important to stay in touch with Him and seek His guidance.

"Behold, the Lord's hand is not shortened, that it cannot save, or his ear dull, that it cannot hear; but your iniquities have made a separation between you and your God, and your sins have hidden his face from you so that he does not hear" (Isa. 59:1-2). As you can see, our sins hinder our prayer lives where we are unable to hear God clearly. But, when freedom comes, we can hear Him. Our Heavenly Father says, "Call to me and I will answer you, and will tell you great and hidden things that you have not known" (Jer. 33:3).

I remember when my entangling sin absorbed my thought-life. My prayer life was almost non-existent. When I managed to pray, evil thoughts infiltrated my mind and kept me from concentrating. Our Heavenly Father tells us to call on Him. He already knows our needs, and He is ready to answer our prayers. His answer may not always come right away. In addition, He will not bless us with consistent, answered prayer, if we do not take care of our entangling sin first.

Today, my prayer life is more effective than it was before God put the desire for my entangling sin to death. He can do the same for you. Take time to call on God and let Him know you need His help and guidance, so you may experience the liberty you already have in Christ Jesus.

SOME FACTS ABOUT PRAYER:

- We are to ask, seek, and knock on heaven's door. We are to call on Him and diligently seek Him (Luke 11:9-10).

- Sin can cause our hearts to condemn ourselves. It can also affect our prayer lives. But God is greater than our hearts, and He will never condemn us (1 Jn. 3:19-20, Rom. 8:33).

- If our heart does not condemn us, we have the confidence to approach Him with prayer (1 Jn. 3:21).

- God will answer our prayers if we obey the Lord and do what pleases Him (1 Jn. 3:22).

- When we pray in God's will, we can be confident God hears us. And in doing so, whatever we ask of Him, we will receive (1 Jn. 5:14).

- We are to ask the Lord to allow the Holy Spirit to work in us to remove any desire for our entangling sin (Luke 11:13).

- Consistent, answered prayer is conditional. For instance, First Peter 3:7 says if a man is not in a right relationship his wife, it can hinder his prayers.

- If we remain in our sins, God hides his face and does not hear our prayers (Isa. 59:1-2).

To open the lines of communication and make sure God will answer your prayers, you need to repent and turn from those sins and activities that hinder your communication with God. One night, I sought an elder brother and told him about my sin problem. I never shared what it was, but I let him know I had a problem with an addiction and needed help. My brother turned his Bible to Luke 11:9-13 and read it to me. He said, "Lynn go and ask God to allow the Holy Spirit to work in you to set you free."

So, I did what he said. After praying for several hours into the night, I finally felt a release. While God did not free me then, a peace came over me. Inside, I knew He would permit the Holy Spirit to intervene.

It's time you open your line of communication with God. Call on Him today. Ask Him to allow the Holy Spirit to work in your life and put your sinful desire to death. Let Him know you cannot stop the addiction by your *will*. Tell Him you need the Holy Spirit to kill the desire in you. After praying, believe God will answer the prayer because your words and deeds are well within His will for your life (1 Jn. 5:14-15).

Praying for your freedom is serious business. Get on your knees and fight; fight with all your heart. Cry out to God and keep praying until you know He will answer your prayer. Remember, fighting for your freedom is war. You must plead your case before the Lord and keep your communication line open. He will hear your prayers and act because He wants you to experience your freedom. The Word says when we pray in His will, and our hearts do not condemn us, He will answer our prayers (1 Jn. 3:21).

In the previous chapter, your assignment was to keep from committing your entangling sin for an entire week. Chances are you may have failed. Even if you didn't, the battle in your mind may have made you crazy. I wanted you to see how impotent your *will* is against an enslaving sin.

This week, if you haven't started already, pray for God's deliverance. Ask the Lord not to lead you into temptation but deliver you from the evil one's temptations and accusations. Every time you pray, end by making the same request. When engaging the enemy, through spiritual warfare, ask God to protect your mind and heart. And as a reminder, continue to seek the Lord to give the Holy Spirit the authority to put the desire for your sin to death. Once the desire dies, your victory arrives.

Regarding the progress chart below, mark a "Y" under every day you make it, and an "N" if you were unable to make it without falling to temptation. If you pray and fight in the Spirit, you should do much better this week. Continue the battle for your freedom over the next several weeks. Each line represents a week. Prayerfully, you won't need to fill in all of them.

PROGRESS ACCOUNTABILITY CHART

Monday	Tuesday	Wednesday	Thursday	Friday	Saturday	Sunday

Note: At this point, I recommend reading "Returning to Holiness" by Dr. Gregory Frizzell. You can find it on **http://frizzellministries.org/returning-to-holiness** the book's website. May I caution you not to read this book like a normal book. As you read this book, prayerfully meditate on what the author says about your walk with God. Now, if you study it properly, there will be days you won't be able to get through a paragraph because this book will examine every aspect of your life, including your thought-life. As you read it, you will see how much of the world's ways have crept into your heart and mind. No matter how long it takes, please finish it before you continue this study. Believe me, you will never experience anything like this again, but you will be glad you did. This book will change your life.

ENGAGE THE ENEMY

A FORMIDABLE OPPONENT

> *"He who exercises no forethought but makes light of his opponents is sure to be captured by them."* (TAW 12) *Sun Tzu*

We fight a formidable opponent. Satan has had 6,000 years to prepare for this day. He tripped up Adam and Eve, and he will continue to tempt you if you fail to engage him with God's Word.

When facing Satan, I suggest you begin with prayer before engaging him. Next, you need to examine your heart. If you have unrepentant sin, now is the time to take care of those sins by confessing them and seeking God's forgiveness. Third, ask God to allow the Holy Spirit to work in you. Fourth, seek His guidance and determine in your heart to stand firm and win this battle. Fifth, you must destroy the enemy's assets; those things Satan uses to keep you entrapped. Sixth, never attack at the enemy's strengths. Instead, attack his weaknesses. Finally, ask God to renew your mind and transform your heart, so you may become a vessel of honor—a trusted soldier God can use to carry out His plans through you.

> *"At a critical moment, the leader of an army acts like one who has climbed up a height and then kicks away the ladder behind him."* (TAW) 13 *Sun Tzu*

As a young man, I remember the following saying, "A Marine never retreats; he charges in the opposite direction." When you engage Satan, you must be in it to win. Retreating or compromising your walk is not an option. Victory is the only option we have when engaging the enemy. So, stand firm, be of good courage, and like a Marine, never retreat (1 Cor. 16:13-14).

DESTROYING THE ENEMY'S ASSETS

What are assets? In a battle, they can be additional troops, machine guns, air cover, and other equipment a fighting unit needs to win. Assets include anything an army has at its disposal to defeat the enemy.

For instance, when the Allies, in World War II, stormed a hill or took a beach, they had to first eliminate key enemy assets if they wanted to succeed. The enemy often used pillboxes or areas where large caliber machine guns could fire long-range from a high, fortified position to defend themselves. These pillboxes made it difficult for the Allies to advance, so they had to eliminate them to complete their objective. To accomplish this, Allies used their assets to engage the enemy. These included battleships firing long-range canons to shell an area, air assets such as bombers or fighter planes, and courageous soldiers who risked their lives storming the elevated positions with flamethrowers, grenades and rifle fire to knock out the pillboxes. While many lost their lives storming these hot areas, their heroic actions saved lives and increased the Allies chances for success.

Likewise, before you can advance, you must destroy the enemy's assets. What assets will Satan use to win his battles? They are items he can use to entice you and keep you trapped in your sin. For example, let's say you have a porn addiction. The assets your enemies have at their disposal may include movie channels, magazines, rented videos, strip clubs, and the Internet through your computer, pad, or smartphone. As a trusted soldier, you must knock these out with filters, disconnects or cancelations before you can advance your walk with God.

Note: Regarding a pornographic addiction and computer filters. I'm not a big fan of the tattle-tell filtering systems where an accountability partner receives an e-mail if you fail. This system won't stop you from viewing a bad site, and it places an unnecessary burden on your accountability partner. If you insist on using this filtering system, please do what a brother in Christ did. He had the e-mail sent to his spouse. This makes it difficult to cheat the system.

I like the filters that keep someone from viewing pornographic or suspicious sites. I suggested one to a friend. He installed his software and had a brother set a secret password for him. While this caused my friend some inconvenience, keeping the password from him stopped him from visiting questionable sites.

Other assets include movie channels. If you have these in your home, consider blocking or removing them. In addition, you may want to block certain non-premium channels. If you watch "R" rated or "PG 13" movies, you want to be careful. On the next page make a list of the assets the enemy uses against you. Then, write how you will destroy or neutralize them. Afterward, mark the last column of your asset with the completion date to confirm you finished the task. Remember, once you engage the enemy, failure to knock out the enemy's assets is not an option. So, stand firm and do all you can through Christ to win this war. You can do it.

To help you fill out the table below, let's continue with the pornography addiction example. The asset might be the Internet. You destroy it by cutting it off or adding a filter to block the Web pages. Then date it. Please do this for each asset the devil can use to hinder your freedom.

ENEMY'S ASSET	YOUR ASSET TO PREVENT OR DESTROY THEM	DATE

BATTLE REMINDERS

Previously, we talked about the reason God put our old nature to death. The old nature and the law were one. To free us from law's penalty (death), our old nature had to die to set us free.

In Christ, we have the freedom to walk with God and not remain entangled in our sins. It is up to us to experience this freedom. I suggest you read Romans, Chapter Six until every word in the chapter stands out. When a verse stands out or speaks to you underline it. Do this for a week or two, and you will see the difference. As for the addiction, if God has yet to set you free, continue to ask Him to allow the Holy Spirit to kill the desire for it and free you from your enslaving sin. You will want to keep filling in your PROGRESS ACCOUNTABILITY CHART. Once you are free, watch how God uses you to further His kingdom.

HEDGE OF PROTECTION

By now, you know to destroy Satan's influence over your mind a renewal and transformation must take place within you. This renewal is not your work. It's the work of the Holy Spirit. Not only will God take away any desire for your sin, He will encase your mind with His hands to create a fortified hedge of protection. This hedge will keep Satan's encase your mind with His hands to create a fortified hedge of protection. This hedge will keep Satan's temptations and accusations from reaching your mind again (Job 1).

I found out about this truth while flying home from a business trip on the West Coast. Sitting by the window, and staring at the billowing clouds surrounding the plane, I became curious about my freedom and wondered if I could ever think on my old thoughts again.

After landing, I placed the luggage in my trunk and drove home. By the time I made it home, those old thoughts returned and overwhelmed my mind. Surprised, I fought to rid my mind of them. As I battled, I asked God what happened. He said, "You wanted to know if you could think on those thoughts again. Lynn, Satan never stopped sending them your way. You couldn't hear them because My hands kept them from reaching you."

God taught me a valuable lesson about how His protection works. After feeling foolish for questioning my freedom, I repented and decided never to place my freedom in jeopardy or take it for granted again. Instead of letting my curiosity set me up for another fall, I now seek heavenly things (Col. 3:1-2). By seeking things from above, where Christ sits, we remain focused on what is good and right rather than let our thoughts drift toward evil. Keeping our focus on things above helps us remain free to serve Christ in Spirit and truth.

Today's assignment is to pray through Psalms 32 and 51. Pray through them as if you wrote them to the Lord. As you do, look at the importance David placed on freedom and having a cleansed conscience before God. As you read David's words, let them speak to your heart.

If you finished your assignment, please list some of the points God used to speak to you in Psalms 32 and 51 and meditate on them. Let them fill your heart as you use them to experience your cleansed conscience and transformed life.

YOUR READING ASSIGNMENT

_____

_____

_____

_____

DAY 11

SECURE THE BATTLEFIELD

DO NOT BECOME CARELESS WITH YOUR VICTORY

After a major battle, soldiers knew how important securing the battlefield was to prevent unnecessary deaths from a lone enemy gunman or some booby trapped, dead body. As for you, once the Lord sets you free the battle is not over until you secure the victory. This means you should never let your guard down once you are free. You must know Satan wants to fire the last round or set a trap to trip you and cause you to fall again. Therefore, arm yourself with God's Holy Word and stay alert (1 Cor. 16:13-14).

Because the Holy Spirit secures your mind and heart, you now have the power to stand against Satan and cast out anything he uses to tempt you to sin. You can make this stand because the Lord swept your mind free of your old sinful thoughts and renewed it on Him. In addition, you are no longer standing on sifting sand. Instead, you are standing on the Rock. Jesus said, "Everyone who comes to me and hears my words and does them, I will show you what he is like: he is like a man building a house, who dug deep and laid the foundation on the rock" (Luke 6:47).

When we follow His Word and obey the Lord, we position ourselves to wage war against Satan. By doing this, we fight from a strengthened position; our strong foundation allows us to stand against Satan and defend ourselves with the truth against his attacks.

In Luke 3, the Holy Spirit takes Jesus into the desert to test Him. The devil tempts Jesus three times, but Jesus uses God's Word to defend himself causing Satan's temptations to fail. Confessing the Word will do the same for you. To defeat Satan, invoke the name of Jesus and use the Word of God to defend yourself and the devil will flee.

HUMBLE YOURSELVES BEFORE THE LORD

> *The Word says, "'God opposes the proud, but gives grace to the humble.' Submit yourselves therefore to God. Resist the devil, and he will flee from you" (Jas. 4:7).*
>
> *After the Lord sets you free, you'll discover how much easier it is to resist the devil. You'll resist him by humbling yourself before God or submitting to His Lordship.*

A renewal and transformation must take place if an addict wants free. Getting there is difficult because the object of the addiction becomes their idol. Without knowing it, they blaspheme the Lord with their entangling sins.

Most of us don't know this, but we're guilty of blaspheming the Lord when we show contempt or lack of reverence toward Him. The opposite happens when we humble ourselves before the Lord. In our humility, we revere Him by placing ourselves under His Lordship. Then, when Satan attacks, we find the strength, through resistance and humility, to stand against Satan or one of his demons, in the name of Christ; then we watch Satan, or his demons flee.

James 4:8 holds the key to your victory. It reads, "Draw near to God, and he will draw near to you. Cleanse your hands, you sinners, and purify your hearts, you double-minded." Do you see why you can now stand where it was impossible to do this before? You can do this because you humbled yourself and drew near to God. Doing these allowed God to purify your heart and remove your double-mindedness by trying to serve two masters. You now despise your sin and love the freedom you have in Christ. Once you taste freedom, you'll fight to keep it because you'll never want to lose it again.

SUBJECT EVERYTHING TO THE NEW MAN

After gaining your victory, it's not the time to relax or grow weary in well-doing. Instead, you must remain alert, study the Word, and be ready for anything the demons toss at you. Believe me they hate to lose. You can bet they will try to claw their way back into your life. (Matt. 12:45) [See more on next page].

Once you have freedom, secure it by focusing on Christ and bringing everything into subjection to the new man or the Lord's righteousness. You do not want to disqualify yourself, where you fail to carry out God's plan for your life, nor do you want to look like a hypocrite (1 Cor. 9:26-27).

The Word tells us at some point, you will want to share your testimony with others. When you walk with God and live in freedom, you have a victorious message other struggling addicts will want to hear. Thus, be careful not to become hypocritical in your walk with God. Do what you tell others to do and gain the respect of your peers.

Below, list some scriptures you can use to stand against Satan's attacks. Ask the Lord to reveal these to you:

SCRIPTURE	VERSE SUMMARY

To be effective, you need God's Word. You can fight Satan with an entire verse or a summary of it. God's Word allows you stand on solid ground and firmly position yourself against Satan's attacks.

USING GOD'S WORD TO DEFEAT SATAN

The devil said to him, "If you are the Son of God, tell this stone to become bread." Jesus answered, "It is written: 'Man does not live on bread alone'" (Luke 4:3-4). As you can see, Jesus quoted scripture to ward off temptation. Besides humbling yourself and standing firm against Satan, you need to fight him with God's Word, just as Jesus did. If you do not know the entire scripture and wish to paraphrase it, please preface your remarks with *the Word says, the Lord says,* or *Scripture says.* It's important you attach the Lord's authority, in Word or name, when you make your stance. By doing this, Satan will know you mean business, and he will flee.

OTHER DEFENSIVE TACTICS

I found one of the best tactics is to remember how bad you felt the last time you sinned. When a temptation finds its way into your mind, recall the time you fell, and remember the shame and guilt you felt when you fell. The Word says, "Remember this and stand firm, recall it to mind, you transgressors" (Isa. 46:8).

Focus on Christ and live worthy of His name (Eph. 4:1). I used to tell my children, "Be" careful not to do anything to harm your name, your family's name, or the Lord's name." So, when I feel an urge to sin, I remember Christ and I tell myself, "I don't want to hurt my Lord or take the chance of jeopardizing the work He's given me to do."

My final tactic has to do with studying God's Word and staying in prayer to keep the devil from invading your mind. In Matthew 12:43-44, Jesus talks about what happens when an unclean spirit leaves you. It travels around looking for another host. When it can't find one, it returns only to find your mind cleansed, but not filled. Seeing an opening, he invites other demons to move in with him. While I see no proof where demons can invade and possess God's people, they can trouble us. Therefore, it's important to secure your battlefield or mind. You do this by reading God's Word, praying, and remaining on guard; ready to dispose of any effort to destroy your new-found freedom in Christ. And when you pray, ask the Father not to *lead you into temptation but deliver you from the evil one*. By ending your prayers this way, you'll see the devil's efforts to reclaim you fade away.

DAY 12

AFTER THE VICTORY

Over time, the temptations will cease as God's hedge of protection allows you time to grow in His Word. God's truths will continue to strengthen your breastplate of righteousness and your helmet of salvation. The breastplate protects the heart, and the helmet protects the mind. Couple these with God's hedge of protection, and you have a solid barrier against Satan's attempts to reignite your old desires.

BECOME A LIVING SACRIFICE

"I appeal to you therefore, brothers, by the mercies of God, to present your bodies as a living sacrifice, holy and acceptable to God, which is your spiritual worship" (Rom. 12:1).

Once the Lord sets you free, and you have secured your mind, it's time to walk out your faith. You do this by becoming a living sacrifice, holy and acceptable to Him.

To be a living sacrifice, you become a perfect offering for the Lord. In addition, you choose to walk according to God's Word by obeying His commands. In doing so, you will become someone God can trust and use to carry out His will.

Amos 3:3 says, "Do two walk together, unless they have agreed to meet?" How can two people walk together unless they agree? Likewise, how can we walk with God, unless we honor Him by becoming a living sacrifice, holy and acceptable to Him? Yes, God wants to entrust us with His deeper truths. However, God cannot do this unless we obey Him. When we obey His commands, Jesus calls us "friend." As His friend, Jesus will show what He has learned from the Father. This means He will open His heart and share the deeper truths with you. (John 14:14-15).

WALKING WITH GOD—PSALM 37

Next to the scripture column, please write the main characteristic, for each verse, in the second column. And then note other verses in Psalm 37 you feel speak to you. Psalm 37 gives us an overview of how we are to walk with God. In the third verse, the Word reminds us to trust

God to finish the work He began in us; we can trust God to keep us in His perfect peace; we can trust Him to answer our prayers; and we can trust Him to keep us in His love, provide for our needs, and guide our paths. In the blanks below, note the first nine verses in Psalm 37.

SCRIPTURE	MAIN CHARACTERISTIC

PSALM 37 OVERVIEW

Psalm 37:4 also reminds us to delight in the Lord, and He will give us our heart's desires. What does it mean to delight in Him? *Delight* means *to find extreme satisfaction or take great pleasure in something or someone.* If we *find extreme satisfaction in the Lord and take great pleasure in Him,* He will give us the yearnings from our hearts. Our first need is to have a relationship with Him. Our Lord should be our greatest longing and serving Him our greatest joy. Yes, God places His desires in our heart. When we take great pleasure in Him, He will fulfill our desires.

Next, we are to commit our ways to Him and trust the Lord to carry out His work in us.

If we commit everything we have to Him, He will give us favor and move to bring about His plan and purpose for our life (Psalm 37:5).

In verse 37:7, the Psalmist reminds us to wait on the Lord. This is one of the toughest things for humans to do. We want to hurry the Lord along, instead of waiting on Him. But, when we wait on Him, and prepare for our future, God will bring His plans for us to pass.

In addition, we are not to worry about evil people getting away with sin (Psa. 37:7). Fret not because those who do evil will stand before the Lord one day and punishment will be their reward. Instead, you are to trust in the Lord, and not to fret; for God will prosper you by giving you what you need to bring your work to pass.

Next, God establishes the steps of a righteous person. Let Him establish your steps. He will guide you into all truth and give you peace. He will preserve you and keep you on His path of righteousness. And though you may suffer a momentary setback, the Lord will uphold you by His hand and preserve you forever (Psa. 37:23, 28).

Finally, those who delight in Him will inherit the land. You will inherit all God has for you on earth and in heaven. On earth, the Word says you will inherit the kingdom of God; His peace, joy, power and other fruit of the Spirit are our inheritance on earth. In heaven, He has treasures and crowns waiting for you. Remember, the Lord should be your greatest delight and treasure. Everything you do should be about Him, now, and forevermore.

KNOWING HIS WILL

When we focus on Christ and walk in His ways, God will show us His will for our life. Paul writes, "Do not be conformed to this world, but be transformed by the renewal of your mind, that by testing you may discern what is the will of God, what is good and acceptable and perfect" (Rom. 12:1-2). When God replaces your old thoughts, with His Word, a renewal in the mind takes place. As this continues, your heart will change, and a transformation will begin within. God does this by exchanging your old desires, with His desires for your life. After a while, your friends and others will notice the transformation. You will no longer be the person you once were as God sanctifies you. Meaning, He'll shape you to reflect His holiness and set you apart for a good work; the calling on your life.

Renewal and transformation help us discern what God's will is for our life. There are three parts to His will: One, we must experience a new birth (Good). Next, we become living sacrifices, holy unto the Lord in the way we walk (Acceptable). Last, God places a calling on our lives. This is the one most people seek or think about when considering His will for their lives (Perfect). His perfect or mature will has to do with the kingdom work God pre-planned for us (Eph. 2:10).

Your addiction, the sin the Word calls the *strong man*, has kept you from knowing God's will or plan for your life. Once free, the discernment you gain will allow you to know God's will for your life. In the beginning, you will only see the end game or where He wants to take you (Isa. 46:10). As you mature in your faith, God will reveal more about His plans for you. The key is to remain patient and trust Him to prepare you to finish the task.

GOD WILL CONTINUE TO ADD TO YOUR CALLING

You may not realize it, but God will continue to add to your calling. If you are unable to spot these additions, you may miss what He has for you. In the blanks below, please list the desires of your heart. These desires are not about items you might like to own one day. Instead, they are what you believe God wants you to do with your life. These may include a secular job that honors Him, or a kingdom work He's called you to do.

As you continue to receive additional information about your calling, add it to this list. First write your yearning, then write the verse or verbal message God gave you to confirm the desire in your heart. The first line shows an example from my walk with God where He gave placed in me a desire to teach, and then added to it several years later. Even today, he continues to add to the picture. He did this for Moses, and my guess He will do it for you also. So, stay alert.

Note: Below, list your heart's desire and then the verse God gave you, and the date He gave it to you to plant or confirm the desire in you. If you have other pieces to your work's puzzle, please continue to add to this chart. On the next page, located in the first paragraph, I have some more examples to help you fill out this chart.

HEART'S DESIRE	GOD SHOWED ME	DATE
To write and teach.	Psalm 32:8. I will guide you and instruct in my ways.	January 1986

God gave me a desire to teach. In 1986, He Showed Me: Psalm 32:8, where He promised to "Guide me and instruct me." In 1994, the Lord set me free from an addiction. He then gave me another heart's desire: God called me to "write, and to help set His people free." In 2004, He gave me another heart's desire to start a ministry, "GodFire Revival and Discipleship Outreach."

Hopefully, these will give you some ideas, so you can spot when He gives you a new heart's desire. What is interesting is how each heart's desire tends to build on the previous ones. Please, continue to jot them down as He shows you more pieces to your calling's puzzle. You may need to make your own chart if you have more desires than blanks.

MENTORING OTHERS

When you gain more knowledge, you will want to pass along what you learn to others. We call this mentoring or discipleship. God may call you to teach God's Word to other believers. Paul wrote the following to Timothy. He said, "and what you have heard from me in the presence of many witnesses entrust to faithful men who will be able to teach others also" (2 Tim. 2:2). Our ministry has several courses available to help you grow in your faith and learn how to teach others. Just visit our website: www.teachthefaithful.org

SCRIPTURE VERSE	LOVE IS/IS NOT

LOVE ONE ANOTHER

In First Corinthians 13, Paul describes what love is and what it is not. Please list them, in the chart above. I find the more we love the deeper God takes us in our walk with Him. So, let God pour His love through you. People will notice, and God will receive the glory.

EPILOGUE

By now, you see the commitment it takes to experience your freedom. Freedom is not just a word we banter around; it's a way of life. We walk in freedom, so we might honor Christ in all we do.

Freedom opens our eyes to the kingdom possibilities God has for us. It sets our hearts free and allows us to think on good thoughts. This freedom gives us hope and inspires us to do great things for God. Because of our freedom, we can focus on Christ and thank Him for freeing us from the guilt, shame, and condemnation our sin caused us to feel inside.

As you know, Satan is a liar. The Bible calls Satan the "accuser" of the saints. Revelation 12:10 describes him as the one who stands before God and accuses the saints. In Zechariah 3:1-3 we read, "Then he showed me Joshua the high priest standing before the angel of the Lord, and Satan standing at his right hand to accuse him. And the Lord said to Satan, the Lord rebuke you, O Satan! The Lord who has chosen Jerusalem rebuke you! Is not this a brand plucked from the fire?"

There is no place for double jeopardy in God's kingdom. Once God frees us from an entangling sin, Satan cannot argue the case before God again. It's over. Even if we fail, and fall to the same sin, Satan cannot accuse us before God nor can he accuse us in our minds regarding our sin. We are free.

What happens if you fall after the Lord sets you free? This may happen to you if it hasn't happened already. This doesn't mean you have lost your freedom. Why? Before, the Lord set you free, you felt compelled to sin; now you know better. This time, your desire played no part in your sin. Instead, you made the choice to sin.

So, use this to your advantage. How? The next time you think about doing it again, think how awful you felt and ask yourself, "Do you want to feel this way again." You will be amazed how this helps to kill the feeling, so you can remain on the right track. You now have the power within to stand against your sin or stop it before it starts. This power was not evident before the Lord removed the desire and set you free, but it is now. Therefore, stand on God's Word, in the name of the Lord Jesus, and watch Satan run.

If you fall again, repent, and then remember how bad it made you feel. The Bible tells us when we sin, after the Lord sets us free, we are like dogs returning to our vomit (2 Pe. 2:22). You will have no pleasure in your sin. It's like vomit. Just remember the moment and sin no more.

Thank you for taking this course. I pray God used it to help you find your freedom. I also pray you'll never want to return to your old sin because freedom in Christ satisfies the heart.

God Bless.

NOTES

[1] Source for both Sample Mission Statements: http://www.missionstatements.com/personal_mission_statements.html, includes both Pat Robertson's and Louise Moranti's Mission Statement

[2] TAW Quote Source: Tzu, Sun, *The Art of War*, p. 11, Copyright 2007, BN Publishing

[3,4,5,6] Wilmington, H. L., *Wilmington's Guide to the Bible,* pg. 756-774, Copyright 1981, 1984 Tyndale House Publishing

[7-8] TAW Quote Source: Sun Tzu, *The Art of War*, pg. 21, 20, Copyright 2007, BN Publishing

[9] TAW Quote Source: Sun Tzu, *The Art of War*, pg. 53, Copyright 2007, BN Publishing

[10] TAW Quote Source: Sun TZU, *The Art of War*, pg. 7, Copyright 2007, BN Publishing

[11] TAW Quote Source: Sun Tzu, *The Art of War*, pg. 45, Copyright 2007, BN Publishing

[12] TAW Quote Source: Sun Tzu, *The Art of War*, pg. 26, Copyright 2007, BN Publishing

[13] TAW Quote Source: Sun Tzu, *The Art of War*, pg.55 Copyright 2007, BN Publishing

TESTIMONIAL

In the beginning of the class of *Battle Plans* by Lynn E. Sheldon, I was totally immersed knowing that I have a real purpose in my life. When we as Christians put on our spiritual armor an arm ourselves with spiritual weapons we can overcome and defeat Satan's dark forces. I also learned much more about myself and God's plans for me. I also know that the biggest battle is in the mind. I learned that I was not a mistake that I'm fearfully and wonderfully made.

I especially like the charts on characteristics, prayers, strengths and weaknesses. They've helped me to see how much I've progressed, and the areas I still need to work on. The same thing goes for Satan's strengths and weaknesses. Praying and fighting for my freedom is definitely spiritual warfare. And I've learned not to be careless with God's love.

I've always been humble before God, especially when I pray to the point of crying; which I should not be ashamed of in any way. The Bible says I'm supposed to be, but I didn't know that until I read "Battle Plans." If I continue to put into practice, the things God has planned for me, the many temptations will eventually cease and God's hedge of protection will cover me as I continue to grow and strengthen in my walk with God.

I absolutely love the book, and will keep it always to refer back to and from time-to-time and hopefully teach my child and her children and generations to come.

Thanks again.

Lisa

Your Sister in Christ.

ABOUT THE AUTHOR

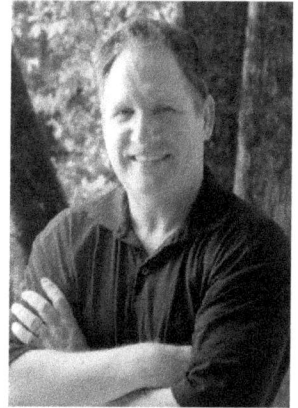

Lynn is both a minister and a student of God's Word and dedicated to teaching the body of Christ. He currently serves as President of GodFire Revival and Discipleship Outreach. This study reflects what he learned while struggling to experience his freedom in Christ. Written in 2011, the information found in Battle Plans has helped many believers experience their freedom from their addiction.

Lynn is the author of *Crucified with Him, No More Namby Pamby,* and *Ambassadors.* Currently, he is developing other studies to serve the body of Christ. Over twenty years ago, Lynn made a promise to his mentor, Dr. Claude Townsend. He assured Dr. Townsend he would teach others what he learned from him. Lynn continues to keep the promise he made thirty-one years ago.

To contact Lynn:

Email: godfire@disciples.com

Web: teachthefaithful.org